VISION POWER

Learning to become a visionary leader

Dr. Albert Zandvoort

CONTENTS

How to use this book

Numerous companies and individuals have already found new routes to success with the concepts and tools presented in this book.

This step-by-step guide is designed to help you to understand yourself better. It's about you, and only about you. It doesn't involve making comparisons with other people, and there are no right or wrong answers. You can work through the guide again at any time if you want to fine-tune the skills you've learned.

The book includes lots of exercises, which involve your filling in the answers to questions after some serious reflection. By the time you've finished, you'll have created your own personal guide to future success as an individual and as a leader.

You'll learn a series of easily understood concepts which will introduce you to the secrets of motivation.

You'll also learn to create a clear vision of where you and your organization are going, and use this as a motivational tool.

And I'll help you to motivate other people to help them achieve your goals.

You'll find the guide often refers to "companies" or "teams", but this guide is designed for anybody who works with other people — whether they work for a company, some other organization, or are self-employed. It's personal to you, and the process of building visions is the same whoever and wherever you are.

At the end of each chapter, you'll find a summary of the main points and learning objectives it contains.

Finally, a word of encouragement. If you're to achieve lasting success, you must make sure you put your visions into practice on a consistent, regular basis. I wish you every good fortune and happiness in doing so.

Introduction

Every person has an inner essence, which defines their existence as an individual: the self.

The self lies at the center of the way we think and feel. It can be seen as the answer to the question "Who am I?" This might sound like a very simple question, but very few people truly know the answer, and most of us spend large parts of our lives in search of our true selves.

Also, a lot of people don't know what they really want out of life. As a result, they do things without knowing whether they really want to or not.

Often, what people do is determined by outside influences, so they end up doing things which aren't important to them or which they don't want to do. If your life is to be meaningful, you need to be at one with yourself, not tossed hither and thither by external circumstances.

In his book Freedom to learn, the famous psychologist Carl Rogers writes: "As soon as a person begins to live from the center of his self, he is freed and ceases to be a chess piece manipulated by others. But this does not mean that his behavior is not influenced by other people or outside circumstances. Rather, the difference lies in the fact that the self is no longer a victim of circumstances, but decides what influences it will admit. In this way the self is free to determine its own destiny and move towards self-realization."

Every person has specific relationships with themselves and other people, and often makes decisions that affect others.

These decisions can lead to self-realization or self-destruction, and if you're to avoid the latter, it's very important to know your self. You must have a knowledge of who you are, what you want and what is important to you if you're to guide other people in a specific direction.

The influence you exert on other people can be positive or negative. If you want to ensure it's not negative, you need to know and understand your own self as well as theirs. Only when you understand other people's selves can you realize your own.

"The most difficult thing in life is... to know oneself"

Thales

In any team situation, the leader and the team members must have achieved a high level of self-awareness if they are to make full use of their potential and want to work effectively towards achieving the team's objectives.

Before you can do this, you'll need to know the answers to the following questions:

- How does the self develop?

- How does our image of ourselves develop?

- How does self-esteem develop?

- How does your self-esteem affect your behavior?

- How do you develop strong self-esteem?

- How does strong self-esteem affect the way you deal with your fellow humans?

- And, central to this book : What is a Vision?

- The first question we need to answer is what is a vision?

Vision derives from the Latin word videre, meaning, "to see". It means a number of different things: one is the sense of sight which we use to perceive the world around us, and another is a sight seen in a dream or trance. But we will be using it in the sense of a mental view or image of something that has the potential to exist in the future. A visionary is a person who can imagine something happening, and has innovative and creative ideas about a reality that does not yet exist, but could do so.

Before a change can take place in the world, it must first take place in the human soul.

Leo Tolstoy

1 - How does your Self-Image develop?

This chapter will help you to carry out an assessment of yourself. All successful people have a relatively accurate picture of themselves and the way they've developed.

Once you become aware of what your true self is like, you will be able to understand the role of hereditary and environmental influences in its evolution.

There is a close relationship between what we call personality and self-image. We ask ourselves questions like: "Who am I? How am I? How did I get like this? Will I always be like this?" We learn a lot about our selves during the course of our lives, and are able to put some of this knowledge to good use. But first of all, we need to acknowledge the self.

In the words of Harvard professor Jerome Kagan, "The main characteristic of life is change."

We're now going to try and understand what your self currently is, and what you would like it to be in the future. Throughout this process, you need to be very open and honest with yourself.

1.1 How the self develops

There are two main factors which help to determine how the self develops:

- Hereditary factors

- Environmental factors

1.2 Hereditary factors

I am reminded of your sincere faith, the faith that dwelt first in your grandmother Lois and your mother Eunice and now, I am sure, dwells in you."

Second Letter of St Paul to St Timothy, 1,5

Many of your characteristics are ones which can be traced back to your ancestors. The most obvious is probably your appearance: you've probably heard people saying: "He looks just like his father/mother/grandfather/uncle".

Newborn babies do actually look more like their fathers than their mothers. This is a clever trick on the part of mother nature: in times when humans did not fully understand the finer points of genetics, the resemblance would have helped to create a bond between father and child and thus ensure that it was protected and looked after.

"She's so obstinate — just like her uncle."

"He's clever — but then so was his grandfather."

"His mother was scatterbrained, and he's followed in her footsteps."

"She very musical. She gets it from her father."

And so it goes on.

Statements like these show that many characteristics can be seen as hereditary. Over the generations, this can mean that whole families and even nations have character traits in common. Think of statements like these:

"The Rothschilds have always had a flair for business."

"The Italians are extroverts."

"Brazilians love dancing the samba."

Exercise 1: Hereditary factors:

1. Think of as many instances as possible where you've been compared to your relatives: mother, father, grandmothers, grandfathers, uncles, aunts, brothers, sisters, sons, daughters.

Example: "You're so outgoing, just like your father".

a)

b)

c)

d)

e)

2.   List the most distinctive features of your appearance, skills and personality. Work out how many of these also apply to other family members.

Characteristic	Family member
E.g. Introverted	Grandfather

3.   How have these different characteristics influenced you...

In your personal life?

At work?

Are any of these answers ones where you thought: Ah, I'd never considered that before? If so, make a note of these here.

1.3 Environmental influences

The environment in which you grow up has a permanent, lifelong effect on the way you are now. The main environmental factors affecting the development of the self include:

- Parents
- School/college/university
- Friends
- Home environment
- Working environment
- Experiences
- Upbringing
- Cultural and religious background

Of course, there are lots of other factors that have made you what you are today. Think of the following:

Early environmental influences and experiences have more effect on the development of the self than those occurring at a later stage in life.

Many of the influences which have helped to shape you may long since have been forgotten, but they're still there.

Experiences and events often have a much more lasting effect than you consciously realize.

Past experiences often influence your development in ways which apparently have nothing to do with the original experience.

The current state of your self is the sum of all your past experiences.

Exercise 2: Environmental influences:

Think about all the environmental factors mentioned in the previous section. For each one, try to identify two important ways in which they've personally influenced you.

Answer this section based on your memory of situations.

a) Your parents

Example: My parents taught me always to be on time.

1. _____

_____

_____

_____

2. _____

_____

_____

_____

b) Your school/college/university

Example: If you're different from the rest of the group, the group will reject you.

1. _____

_____

_____

_____

2. _____

_____

_____

_____

c) Your friends

Example: Good friends are always there when I need them most.

1.

2.

d) Your home environment

Example: People don't look after each other enough.

1.

2.

e) Your working environment

Example: Your value is determined by your place in the hierarchy.

1.

2.

f) Your experiences

Example: Life has taught me that you can't rely on anyone but yourself.

1.

2.

g) Your cultural and religious background

Example: Do unto others as you would wish to be done by.

1.

2.

Choose any five of the above statements at random. Describe how they affect your everyday life today.

For example, the way 2b) — school, college or university — has affected you is that you don't easily bow to group pressure.

a

b.

c.

_____

_____

_____

_____

d.

_____

_____

_____

_____

e.

_____

_____

_____

_____

1.4 Nature versus nurture –what are your choices?

The debate about the role of hereditary and environmental factors in human development was perhaps most pithily summed up by Francis Galton in the 19th century: "nature versus nurture".

Inheritance or the environment — which is it that makes us unique? The answer to this question depends on the extent to which you feel responsible for your attitudes and actions.

Behaviorism is based on the assumption that man comes into the world more or less as a blank slate, and his character is determined by his upbringing and experiences. On the other hand, in 1993 Dean Hamer of the National Institute of Health in Washington DC made headlines after claiming to have discovered the gay gene. And Thomas Borcher, famous for his pioneering studies of twins, says cautiously: "Genes aren't rules, they're options. For example, thanks to better diet we're getting increasingly tall, but that doesn't mean our genes have changed."

2 - Finding the core of your leadership self

One of the central questions in any whodunit is why the killer should have wanted to commit the murder in the first place. What was his motivation? Everything we do, and the way we behave in any given situation is determined by our motivations; you could call them the core questions of our existence.

In this chapter, you'll learn to recognize what motivates you personally.

You can't create a vision of success until you know what your motivations in life are.

2.1 What makes you tick?

Every human being has a central motivation, even if it's an unconscious one. It's what gives purpose to your life, makes you aware of what your goals are, and gives you your drive.

Motivation can also be seen as what makes you happy and determines your quality of life. And of course it's different for each person. Some may be motivated by religion, others by social status, power or wealth. Since it's your main source of energy, you should know what you expect from life.

This might sound strange, but in fact very few people know what they want out of their existence. This is because it's normally imprinted on you during childhood, when your mother and father have a major influence on you. This may result in the development of motivation which does not lead to self-realization.

2.2 Barriers to self-realization

The following factors often act as barriers to self-realization:

- Parents' motivations
- Parents' ideals and expectations
- The community's expectations
- The community's ideals and ethics
- The community's accepted norms
- Moral values
- Group pressure
- Social order
- The influence of school, college etc.
- A reaction against one or more of the above factors

True self-realization is achieved when your motivation is based on making a meaningful contribution to society using your own specific gifts and potential. Such motivations could be described as a vision.

This vision is the understanding of the influence you can exercise when you make full use of your potential. Motivation based on such a vision leads to self-realization, and also makes a significant contribution to your quality of life. That's why everyone should be fully aware of their motivations, and exercise 3 helps you to do this.

The key to self-management is the ability to observe oneself. It is important to realize that self-observation is not the same as overly negative criticism, condemnation or paralysis by analysis. Rather, it is constant observation of one's own performance from an outside perspective that allows an accurate evaluation to be made.

Charles A. Garfield: Peak performers. The new heroes of American business.

Of course, this is an exclusive process of looking at yourself, your self-image. You can see only fragments of other people's images of you, and only by observing yourself over a long period and reflecting critically on your values, objectives and visions.

You can get an honest external picture of yourself from a good friend, though it may not be a complete one. It's better to obtain constant feedback from a variety of people who know , and best of all is to use a good personal coach.

Exercise 3: Identify your motivation:

Answer the following questions. If you reply honestly, this exercise will give you a clearer idea of what motivates you.

a) List the three to five cleverest/stupidest things you've done in your life.

b) Why are these the cleverest/stupidest things you've ever done?

c) How would you describe a good/bad day in your life?

d) What do you want to achieve in your life?

Answer this question by completing the following sentence: "At the end of my life, I'd like to be able to say..."

e) Decide what your motivation is on the basis of the information you've given in the previous questions, and write it down.

_____
_____
_____
_____

f) Test your motivation using the ten bullet points at the beginning of section 2.2.

_____
_____
_____
_____

Is this really what you want out of life?

_____
_____
_____
_____

2.3 Living out your motivation

To what extent are you realizing your motivation in the different areas of your life — for example at work, and in your spiritual, social, political and financial life? Write your motivation in the inner circle of the diagram below, and use the 5-point scale to show how far you're realizing it in the different areas of your life. Draw a line joining up the points to see how far your life matches your motivation. The outer circle represents 100%; in other words you're achieving maximum realization in that particular area of your life.

The lowest value, 0, is in the center of the circle, and the highest, 5, is on the edge. You could also copy the circle and use it to assess the extent to which you're achieving self-realization in any other area of your life.

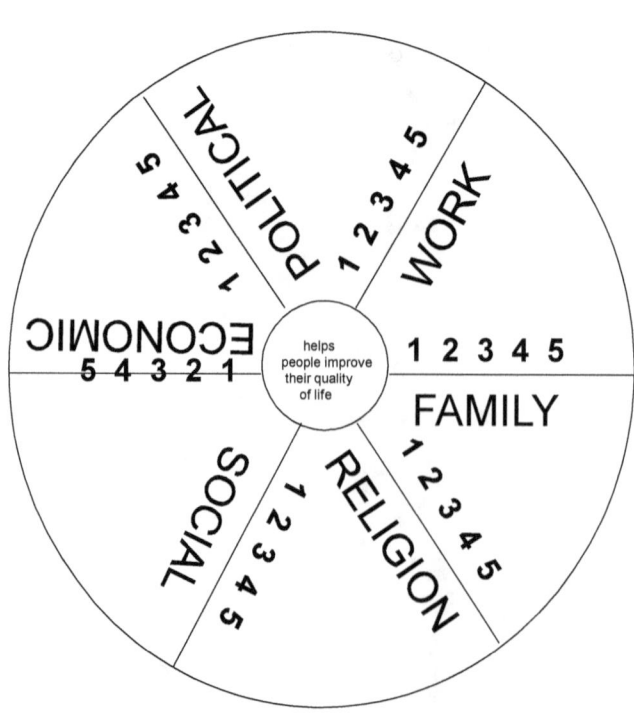

The areas between the line you've drawn and the outside of the circle show where you could achieve greater self-realization.

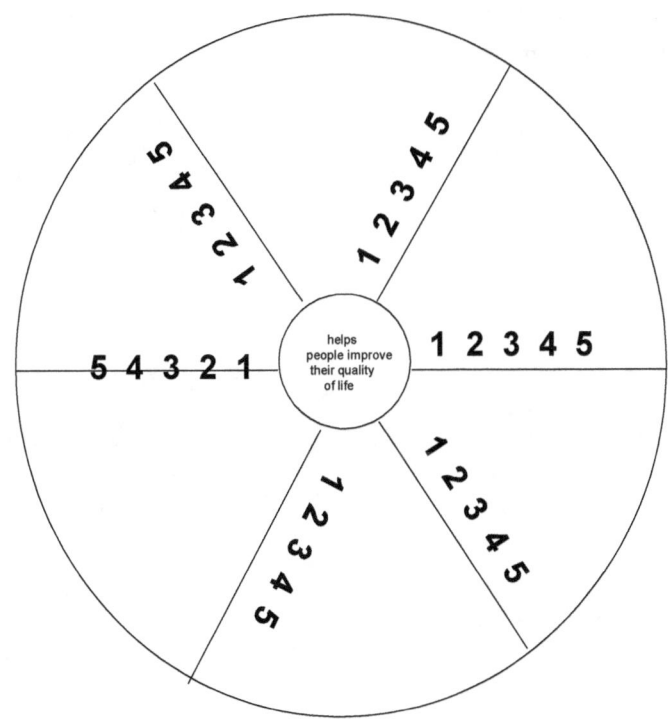

helps people improve their quality of life

Every psychological extreme conceals its own opposite or has a deep-seated, real relationship with it... there is no sanctified tradition which cannot occasionally change into its opposite, and the more extreme a position is, the more easily we can expect it to be transformed into its opposite.

Carl Gustav Jung

Exercise 4: Activate your potential:

For each of the six axes of the circle of motivation, write down something you could realistically do to realize your motivation more strongly. Generally speaking, it's better to expand your potential in a number of small, realistic steps than to set unrealistic goals, or ones which cannot be achieved all in one go.

a

b.

c.

d.

e.

Do this exercise again whenever you've achieved your objectives.

2.4 Summary of chapters 1 and 2

If you are to know and understand yourself, you need to know how your self has developed. Although your current self is largely a product of your background, nobody should ever be a victim of their own past.

You have the ability to transcend your circumstances and shape your own future, provided you do the following:

- Don't see yourself as a victim of fate and unable to influence your destiny.

- Accept who you are, and devote your energy to making full use of your potential. Bear in mind that most people achieve only a small part of what they're capable of; Einstein said it was just 20%. That's why the amount of potential you have is less important than what you make of it.

- Be fully aware of what you want out of life, ensure that your motivation matches this, and take action in as many areas of your life as possible in order to realize yourself.

Experience is not what happens to a person. It is what a person makes out of what happens to them.

Aldous Huxley

3 - From knowing yourself to appreciating yourself

A successful person can use their self-image and self-awareness to increase their self-esteem.

In this chapter, you'll learn to build on your initial understanding of yourself and to take a holistic view of your personality.

Personal and business success can often be achieved only with the support of a team. This chapter also deals with some first principles for working with teams.

A team may be a network, a partnership, or any other group of people in your work or home life.

3.1 What we mean by self-image and self-esteem

Self-image

The term "self-image" is self-explanatory: it's the picture you have of yourself, like a mirror image. Just as a mirror gives an objective, value-free picture, so your self-image should not be judgmental in any way, but purely a description of your self.

Self-image has a number of different dimensions. The following are the most important in a work environment:

- Personality
- Skills
- Values
- Attitudes
- Appearance
- Presence

If you are to be successful, you need to know how to mobilize the above factors for your own benefit and the benefit of the team. This means you must know not only your own self-image, but also try to discover that of every team member.

Self-esteem

Your self-esteem is what you think and feel about your self-image. It involves coming to a judgment, which may be positive or negative. If you're generally satisfied with your self-image, you're probably have a high sense of self-esteem — and vice versa.

3.2 Personality: a jigsaw with countless parts

Personality is a combination of different and inherent characteristics or preferences that influence human behavior. One of the most important is your ability to survive, your psychological resilience. This is a characteristic of primary importance for visionary leadership, and results from the interaction between other traits. There are a number of different models for describing and analyzing these (see also 2.2).

The table in exercise 5 contains a series of relatively abstract characteristics. Think about each of these, and decide where you fit in between the two extremes.

Exercise 5: Personality:

Extroverted	5 4 3 2 1 0 1 2 3 4 5	Introverted
Organized	5 4 3 2 1 0 1 2 3 4 5	Disorganized
Feeling	5 4 3 2 1 0 1 2 3 4 5	Thinking
Intuitive	5 4 3 2 1 0 1 2 3 4 5	Analytical
Holistic	5 4 3 2 1 0 1 2 3 4 5	Focused on detail
Practical	5 4 3 2 1 0 1 2 3 4 5	Impractical

It may be that you're not satisfied with your assessment of yourself. However, this exercise is not about being satisfied or dissatisfied: it's about identifying individual aspects or characteristics and how you deal with them.

What do you think about your personality? Which aspects do you feel positive about, and which negative?

Positive:

Negative:

3.3 Skills : No one can do everything

Everyone has specific strengths and weaknesses. It's vital that you have a realistic picture of your skills and use them to the best advantage. You also need to be able to identify and use the skills that exist within your team.

As no one is likely to combine all the skills you need to put your visions into practice, it's very important to put together a supporting team that covers a broad range of knowledge and experience.

If we are to create futures, we must find new forms of community.

Antoine de Saint-Exupéry

Exercise 6: Strengths and weaknesses:

List your main strengths and weaknesses.

Write down how you feel about each one.

Main strengths	Feeling
E.g. Good communicator	Good
a)	
b)	
c)	

Main weaknesses	Feeling
E.g. Not a good listener	Guilty
a)	
b)	
c)	

3.4 Values

Values are specific assumptions about the core issues that are important if a team is to achieve its objectives. A shared system of values is essential if the team is to work together effectively. This means that all members must share the same values, be willing to uphold them and know what will happen if they fail to observe them.

Values are also an important component of individual self-image. Conflicting values within a team can adversely affect the way in which it seeks to attain its objectives. Relations within the team can also be harmed if its values are significantly different from those of some of its members.

You should therefore frame your specific personal values, such as punctuality, within the context of more generalized values such as reliability, so that yours are in tune with those of the team. This is particularly important when new members join the team.

Water is flowing, gentle and adaptable.

But it is able to wear down the hard, unyielding rock. This is another paradox: in gentleness lies strength.

Laotse

Exercise 7: Values:

Which personal values are important to you (e.g. honesty, consideration for others)?

Negative:

Which values are important to the team that you manage or belong to?

How do your personal values differ from those of the team? How do you feel about this?

3.5 Attitudes

Your attitudes are expressed in particular modes of behavior in your working and home life, the way you deal with other people, and your values and management style. Your attitude towards other people shows whether you:

- Accept or reject the way they behave
- Believe in them or not
- Are willing to expend energy on them
- Know what you want to achieve
- Are motivated in particular situations

Attitudes are an important component of your self-image, as they determine your behavior to a large extent. It's therefore very important that you decide what your attitude is towards the key elements of the system in which you work.

Loving oneself also means loving others.

Sonaya Roman

Exercise 8: Attitudes:

Imagine some situations in which you play a leadership role, for example in an organization or among friends and family. Try to describe your attitudes towards the aspects listed below. How do you feel about these attitudes?

a) Your team's objectives

Feelings:

b) The other team members

Feelings:

c) The organization as a whole

Feelings:

d) Yourself

Feelings:

3.6 Physical appearance

Your appearance is an important part of your self-image. It's extraordinary how the way other people interact with you is conditioned by the way you look. Important aspects of appearance include height, weight, facial features, and clothing.

Your appearance also says something about the degree to which you adhere to group norms and your relationships with other people. Wearing a business suit, a punk outfit or a traditional costume are all expressions of the peer group to which you belong.

Exercise 9: Appearance:

Briefly describe your appearance

What do you think about your appearance?

3.7 Presence

Your presence is also an important part of your self-image. The way you interact with those around you is affected by such factors as your body language, your speech and gestures, and the loudness of your voice. These reflect the way you see yourself and your mood at that particular time.

Some aspects of appearance are also the subject of false stereotypes; for example some people still believe that blondes are unintelligent and redheads have fiery personalities.

But these preconceptions ultimately tell us nothing about the person's true self.

Returning to your body means returning to your true nature.

Kurt Bendin

Exercise 10: Your presence:

Briefly describe your presence

What do you think of your presence?

How do you feel about your presence?

3.8 Summary of chapter 3

Your self-image is a subjective assessment. It is determined by your origin, your social environment and your motivations. It is a combination of hereditary factors and of what you have learned and experienced at this point in your life. It cannot change overnight, though it can change gradually as you learn and experience new things and your motivations change. However, your priority at the moment is to understand and accept your current self-image, so it's important to be aware of the following points:

- You are the image you have of yourself, and it is all you have.

- You can only be yourself and not anyone else. It is therefore important that you accept yourself.

- Your self is a unique combination of factors. There is unlikely to be anyone else who's exactly the same as you. Every person is one of a kind.

- Because you're unique, you play a unique role in society. No one else can play your role.

- Because of this, regardless of your status, you have the same value as any other person. You can only lose this value by not realizing yourself to the fullest extent.

- Self-realization allows you to make full use of your potential and play your specific role in society. Without it, your destiny will remain unfulfilled.

- Everyone has an equally valuable role to play. Your task is to create the circumstances in which you and your fellow team members can achieve full self-realization.

- Self-esteem :Self-image as a means of self-realization

- The past is the past, and you can't change it. That's why you need to have a positive attitude towards your self, and regard it as a collection of possibilities and opportunities, not impossibilities and barriers.

- Take control of your own destiny. Decide what you want your future self-image to be, and then create the circumstances and environment you need to achieve it.

- People with low self-esteem spend too much time thinking about the past. People with high self-esteem accept the past, including the mistakes they've made, and use their energy to create a new future for themselves.

Understanding others' behavior requires intelligence. But understanding oneself requires wisdom.

Laotse

4 - Developing the leadership brain

4.1 The cognitive process: The importance of being solution-focused

Your feeling of self-esteem is determined partly by emotional factors and partly by cognitive ones, in other words the way in which you think about and perceive yourself. The cognitive process occurs when you receive information about yourself from your own and others' perceptions, and from interacting with other people.

If this information generates negative thoughts and feelings about yourself, the result is low self-esteem. If they are positive, however, you are likely to feel a high sense of self-esteem.

Nearly all cognitive information can be processed and reinforced in a positive or negative way — it's all down to you. This means that self-esteem is also dependent on the way in which you assess things that happen to you.

4.1.1 Reactions to cognitive information

In each of the following situations, there are two ways in which you can react:

You fail an exam:

I'm a total failure, I'll never pass.

or

Now that I know what the exam is like and which areas I didn't do enough work on, I'll pass next time round.

Someone compliments you on your appearance:

He's trying to butter me up.

or

He's right, I'm looking good and I'm well-dressed.

You have a car crash:

Damn, my car's a write-off.

or

Thank God nobody's hurt.

Someone points out a mistake you've made:

He's just trying to undermine me (or, alternatively, I'm simply no good).

or

He's just pointing out my weaknesses and telling me how I can improve.

Add some examples of your own:

a.

b.

c.

4.1.2 How your responses affect your self-image : A constant, endless cycle

The way in which you think about yourself constantly influences your self-image. Each time you have a positive or negative thought, it becomes an integral part of your existing self-image.

If you interpret everything that happens to you in a negative way, you'll inevitably end up having low self-esteem. Conversely, a constant flow of positive thoughts will result in high self-esteem. At the same time, low self-esteem generates negative thoughts and high self-esteem creates positive thoughts. This leads to a negative or positive cycle, as follows:

Positive cycle

Perception	$\Rightarrow$	*Positive thoughts*
	$\Downarrow$	
High self-esteem	$\Rightarrow$	*Become part of self-image*

Negative cycle

Perception	$\Rightarrow$	*Negative thoughts*
	$\Downarrow$	
Low self-esteem	$\Rightarrow$	*Become part of self-image*

Exercise 11: Thought processes:

1. List five common situations that make you feel negative about yourself, and say why.

Example:

When someone gives me negative feedback...

... I take it as a personal criticism of me.

which cannot be achieved all in one go.

a

b.

c.

d.

e.

2. Write down how you could take a more positive view of the above situations.

Example: When I receive negative feedback about my work...

... I regard it as information that I can use to improve myself.

which cannot be achieved all in one go.

a

b.

c.

d.

e.

3. Next time any of these situations occurs, see it in a positive light, thereby replacing a negative cycle with a positive one.

4.2 Cognitive dissonance : The difference between our real and ideal selves

All the time, consciously or unconsciously, you're working on developing and reassessing your self-image and building high or low self-esteem. Ultimately, this results in an ideal vision of the self. As you become aware of the difference between your current and ideal self-images, a cognitive dissonance is created and you seek to narrow the gap between the two.

Cognitive dissonance can arise whether your self-esteem is high or low. If it's low, the dissonance may arise in areas such as the following:

- The past
- Your mistakes
- Your shortcomings
- Your failures
- Your limitations
- Your lack of certain skills

In cases like these, you're likely to focus your energies on remedying your weaknesses and avoiding change.

If you have high self-esteem, cognitive dissonance can be caused by factors such as the following:

- Visions
- Solutions to problems
- Future possibilities
- Existing potential
- Expectations
- Skills

If you're such a person, you probably accept your current situation and spend very little time and energy trying to remedy past mistakes.

Instead, you concentrate on implementing your vision of the future and achieving self-realization.

A suitably skilled personal coach can help to bring out cognitive dissonances that you're unaware of.

4.3 Summary of chapter 4

How you react to a particular event obviously depends partly on your emotional situation at the time. Feelings like anger or fear can often prevent you from thinking clearly, and disrupt the cognitive process.

It's important to learn how to use the process of cognitive reinforcement described above, and to do so automatically. It will help you to ensure that such things as fear of failure, impatience, and inability to control your anger do not affect your positive cognitive process.

5 - How your self-esteem affects your leadership

This brief chapter provides the theoretical knowledge you need to increase your self-esteem in practice and achieve the desired success.

5.1 How self-esteem affects behavior

One symptom of low self-esteem is procrastination: you rarely do anything new or different because you lack self-confidence. Your procrastination threshold depends on many factors.

This module takes a detailed look at the various ways in which your self-esteem influences your behavior, using some rather extreme examples. As you read it, try to think of similar instances from your own life.

5.1.1 Positive behavior: Accepting information in a positive spirit

If you have high self-esteem and you receive new information about yourself, you're likely to acknowledge, accept and internalize it.

This doesn't mean that you necessarily regard such information as the truth, but the very fact that you accept it in a positive way will result in positive behavior. If you're such a person, you're likely to be good at the following:

- Taking risks.
- Taking the initiative when necessary
- Encouraging other people
- Exploring new territory
- Giving recognition where it's due
- Not imposing too many rules on yourself or other people

5.1.2 Negative behavior

However, if you've got low self-esteem, the likelihood is that when you receive information that relates to your self-image, you'll deny and block it out.

For example, you're unlikely to see positive or negative feedback as something that is essentially a good thing; it will simply make you feel insecure, anxious and threatened. Negative feelings about self-image are often reflected in behavior patterns such as the following:

- Avoiding risks at all costs
- Defensiveness
- Rule-bound behavior
- Using criticism as a form of defense
- Constantly seeking reassurance
- Acting in a withdrawn manner.

Positive behavior patterns are important for interaction between people, because they are clearly recognized by others. They encourage team members to develop their own image and self-esteem, and thus to achieve greater cohesion as a group.

Positive people create positive groups, and negative people create negative groups.

So self-esteem is the key variable in your success. If you're to be truly successful, you need continuously to develop your self-esteem.

This doesn't mean you always have to straitjacket yourself into being positive about everything. When somebody dies, for example, it's a tragic event and no one can pretend otherwise.

There is no path that leads to truth.

Truth must be discovered, but there is no formula for discovering it.

If something is formulated, it is not true.

You must be brave enough to push forward into the unknown,

and the unknown is you yourself.

Discoveries bring joy, a joy which is always reborn.

Self-knowledge is the beginning of wisdom,

in whose calm stillness the immeasurable becomes tangible.

Krishnamurti

5.2 Summary of chapter 5

Your self-esteem is the sum of a great variety of factors. The more you're aware of these, the more you'll see the interdependence between self-esteem and behavior. If you're willing to continue along the path of exploration, maybe we can guide you.

6 - Leading others in trust

In the last chapter, we used a combination of theory and exercises to show how you can exert a positive influence on yourself and others.

The most important objective is to build long-term, positive relationships with yourself and the people around you.

Only by dealing responsibly with your own and others' self-esteem can you achieve lasting success.

6.1. Managing yourself and others

Most people think in very narrow ways, and act in accordance not with the truth, but what they perceive to be the truth. Because of this blinkered attitude, they miss out on a great deal of information and make do with half-truths and half-correct or even false beliefs. This is often down to laziness.

6.2 The persuasiveness of vision

But not everyone is willing to accept received wisdom in this way. Take Christopher Columbus who, like Aristotle, Strabo and Seneca before him, dared to take issue with the generally held view that the earth was flat. He sailed westwards seeking a sea route to India — and at about the same time, in 1497, Vasco da Gama sought to do the same thing but in an easterly direction.

Imagine Columbus meeting his bankers; perhaps the conversation went something like this. "Ah, Columbus, these designs for your new ships are very impressive. So where are you planning to go, exactly?" "Er, round the world." "Round the world?" "Yes. You see, I believe the earth is a sphere, so I want to sail round it." There's a long silence as everyone tries to absorb what Columbus has said. And then someone pipes up: "Fine, do what you like, but you're not doing it with our money!"

Fortunately, Queen Isabella I of Castile and Ferdinand II were rather more open-minded than the bankers, and provided Columbus with the money for his expedition in 1492. But his problems were far from over. You can probably imagine the reaction when he tried to recruit a crew. "What did you say? Sail over the edge of the earth? No thanks! If you think the world is round, you're crazy."

These were the kind of attitudes that Columbus had to overcome before he could persuade men to sail with him. He must have had very great persuasive powers.

In 1493, he returned from what he believed was India but was actually the West Indies, on the opposite side of the globe. Ironically, Columbus believed until his death on May 20, 1506 that he'd been to India. He was convinced that the world was round and he had as much nautical knowledge as the next man, but he'd never reckoned with the existence of a continent between Europe and Asia as he sailed west.

You too can overcome your preconceived ideas. And you can even overcome other peoples' — provided you have sufficient vision.

Lots of people see the world from a narrow, limited perspective; in fact, it's not just individuals but whole organizations that are guilty of this. But you need to start by learning how to overcome your own preconceptions.

Next time you're trying to convince other people that there might be other ways of looking at the world, think of Columbus.

Exercise 13: Preconceptions:

Write down five preconceptions other people might have about you.

which cannot be achieved all in one go.

a

b.

c.

d.

e.

Now write down five preconceptions that you've had about other people.

which cannot be achieved all in one go.

a

b.

c.

d.

e.

Next, list five preconceptions that are circulating in your department or organization — including ones about you!

which cannot be achieved all in one go.

a

b.

c.

d.

e.

Now try to hold these preconceptions as just what they are and not as facts!!

If you change the way you think, you're also changing the way you act. If someone tells you something, your unconscious will accept it until a different belief comes along. Even a couple of positive words from somebody else can significantly affect your behavior. Take marriage for example. When your partner says "I do" and the person officiating says, "I now pronounce you man and wife", this can affect the whole of the rest of your life.

And if by any chance the marriage doesn't work out, another rite of passage occurs. The judge says, "I hereby declare this marriage dissolved," and you walk out of the court as a single person again.

There are lots of these simple rites of passage in other areas of life. Sports and leisure are one example. If you're learning to fly a plane, your instructor can change your life simply by saying "Congratulations — you're now a fully qualified pilot".

Life is full of these figures of authority who have a magical ability to change the way you see yourself. Some of them are good magicians, and others are bad ones.

Exercise 14: Figure of authority:

To whom have you ever been a figure of authority? What has been the reaction of the people concerned?

6.3 The power and art of the magician

Dorothy and Toto were making their way through the magical land of Oz, somewhere over the rainbow. They were searching for Kansas, and the good fairy told them: "You must visit the wizard of Oz. He has the power to help you find what you're looking for."

So off they went to see the wonderful wizard of Oz and witness all the wonderful things he could do. After many adventures in the company of a scarecrow, a tin man and a cowardly lion, they found the wizard. In fact he was a bit of a conman, but people believed what he said and that made him into a magician.

He gave the scarecrow a diploma to show that he had brains and was not really stupid. He gave the tin man a clock for a heart to show that he had feelings, and a medal to the cowardly lion to signify that he was brave really.

Such is the power of the magician! In a single action, they can change a person's whole life.

Of course, you've probably met the occasional bad magician who, with a few well-chosen words, can destroy your entire self-confidence - but only if you bother to listen to them.

Magicians never give away their tricks, because they know this would mean the loss of their myths.

William A. Cohen

Exercise 15: Magicians:

List four magicians who've had a major influence on your life.

Make it your aim to be a constructive magician. Give other people courage and confidence — don't take it away from them.

But whether you're a positive or a negative magician, be aware of how much power you have over other people **and over yourself as well!!**

7 - Motivating yourself and those you lead

The only effective motivation comes from within. In this chapter, you'll learn to identify and use the positive tension that is essential for true motivation. You're also seeing the difference between constructive and destructive motivation.

In this and some of the following chapters, you'll find it helpful to have someone to give you feedback. This person might be your coach, a friend or just a person you trust.

7.1 Motivating yourself and others

Motivating yourself involves a constant process of self-persuasion. Motivating others is a more indirect process, which involves persuading them by identifying their objectives and ideas.

7.1.1 What is true motivation?

True motivation comes from inside you. According to gestalt psychology, humans are always in search of inner order.

The ideal image in your unconscious should be identical with your external reality. If these two images are different, you have a problem: you have no inner order.

If you have a picture deep in your unconscious of yourself driving a flashy new car, but your car is actually a clapped-out old wreck, then you have a problem.

This tension between your inner image and the actual reality is generally described as motivation. The bigger the distance between the image and the reality, the greater the drive to resolve the conflict created by your inner tension.

If you want to build a ship, do not summon men together

to fetch wood, make tools ,allocate tasks, but teach people a yearning for the wide, endless sea.

Antoine de Saint-Exupéry

Exercise 16: Creative tension

List five situations where there was a strong tension between your inner picture or vision and the external reality. Discuss with a friend or partner how you dealt with this creative tension.

a

b.

c.

d.

e.

As soon as your inner picture is the same as the external reality, you will lose drive and energy. This means that if you want to remain motivated and full of energy, you must always internalize new objectives and at the same time obtain continuous feedback from the current reality.

7.1.2 Motivating your team members

As an external motivator, all you can do is draw a picture. The members of your team must be able to take this picture as their own and internalize it.

Of course, it's possible that the team members won't have sufficient energy to move reality in the direction of this inner idea or vision. This means you must be able not only to shape and describe the vision yourself, but you should also ask for input from other people so that they can accept it as their own.

Exercise 17: Change:

Identify two things in your personal life that you want to change.

a

b.

Describe one of these things to your partner so that they understand it at a deep level.

Ask your partner for feedback: how far have you succeeded in being persuasive and convincing?

7.2 Types of motivation

As we saw in chapter 4.1.1,anyone can strengthen and internalize their positive or negative thoughts. This also applies to motivating oneself or other people.

7.2.1 Destructive motivation: an example of inappropriate pressure

Destructive motivation is based on such factors as:

- The feeling "I must do it now, otherwise..."
- Fear of something
- Pressure
- Those dreaded words "I ought"

The following scenario shows what happens if you try to pressurize a child into learning to ride a bike. The child gradually starts to get the knack of it, but then falls over and hurts himself. You shout at him because you don't think he's trying hard enough. Under pressure like this, he probably will learn to ride the bike, motivated by the fear of failure and verbal abuse. But if you later try to teach him a couple of new tricks on the bike, he's likely to refuse to cooperate: in his mind, learning has become associated with pain.

A similar kind of thing happens if you put employees under unnecessary pressure. They learn the skills and do the job, but their morale is poor and they perform less effectively than if they'd been taught in a more pleasant, relaxed environment.

You won't succeed by bullying people. You simply have to know how to talk to them.

Lee Iacocca

7.2.2 Constructive motivation: Responsibility through motivation

Constructive motivation is based on such factors as:

- The knowledge that you can do the job, and enjoy it into the bargain.
- The personal advantages that accrue as a result
- Not being under pressure.

The best way to approach anything in life is to say: "I want to do this because I know I'm going to enjoy it." But it's important to take full responsibility for what you expect out of life.

If you say: "I've got to go to work", you're admitting that someone else is in charge of your life. Whenever you say "I've got to..." you're abdicating responsibility.

And each time you say "I ought to...", this reinforces your unconscious idea of yourself as being governed by outside forces beyond your control.

If you go on a diet for the wrong reasons, your unconscious may lead you keep on overeating because its image of you is that of an overweight person. It is defending itself by making it impossible to diet, and giving you lots of justificatory arguments for continuing to overeat.

On the other hand, if you're able to create an image of yourself as being of normal weight, you'll actually want to go on a diet, and the diet will succeed.

You cannot light a fire in another person unless there is one burning in you.

St Augustine

Exercise 18: Motivators:

Think of some situations in which your main motivation was fear, and how this influenced you. Talk to your partner or coach about them.

Think of some examples of cases where you've been constructively motivated and how this influenced you. Again, discuss these with your partner or coach.

Think of some examples of situations when you've used fear to motivate other people. Talk to your learning partner about the effects this had.

Now think of some cases when you've constructively motivated other people. Discuss with your learning partner how you went about this and what the outcome was.

7.3 Familiarity and change: The power of the familiar

For most people, it doesn't matter what kind of an environment they are in, as long as they feel at home in it. The more familiar the environment the better they feel, and if it changes, they will find highly creative ways of restoring or recreating it; this is partly out of laziness.

Some prison inmates become so used to a regulated institutional environment that when they're released, they feel out of place in a free society and commit further crimes so that they can return to prison.

So never forget to prepare for change. A familiar environment can be very restrictive, and can result in some team members opposing growth and change.

An elderly journalist once told me about the wailing and gnashing of teeth that occurred in his office when management replaced typewriters with word processors. The familiar old machines that formed the center of their working lives were taken away from them, and they were given electronic toys that beeped at them and told them what to. Their copy appeared on a screen instead of the familiar sheets of paper.

So where did the managers go wrong? Well, for a start they had failed to prepare staff for drastic change by creating a picture in their minds of what their new workplace would look like. They failed to give them any clear idea of how computers would make their work much easier and quicker, how they would no longer get their hands covered in ink from carbon paper, and how quickly their copy could be rewritten. The journalists did not have the chance to imagine themselves working with a machine that would check their text for spelling mistakes, count the number of words they'd written, and do their page layouts for them. In short, they simply did not realize how much the new machines would improve their quality of life.

As any management consultant will tell you, an ounce of preparation is worth a pound of cure.

Many managers make changes to the working environment without a moment's thought for how this will affect staff. They shift desks and computers around, introduce new procedures and systems and even rebuild whole office blocks. And then they wonder why there's so much resistance from employees and why they're leaving the company in droves. "What's wrong with these people? Don't they know what's good for them?"

It doesn't matter whether the change is for the better or the worse — the simple fact of its occurring is all that's important. If team members aren't given the opportunity to imagine themselves in their new working environment, resistance is inevitable. This can have a serious effect on morale.

All significant, lasting change comes from within.

Familiar surroundings are extremely important to people. If you don't help them to change from within — adapt to new objectives, develop an idea of how new ways of working will affect them and picture the advantages — they'll oppose change because it's being forced on them.

On the other hand, if you can use metaphor and visualization to help them see change in a positive light and feel happy about it, then you'll reap the benefits. This approach takes the stress out of change because team members feel that your objectives are the same as their own.

So don't just take a blind leap out of your familiar environment and expect other people to jump with you. Give them a clear idea, visually, verbally or emotionally, of the qualitative and quantitative outcomes you want to achieve. Set inner goals that people can identify with, not external ones that are imposed on them. And start by creating a picture in your own mind before you try to create one in theirs. If you approach change and growth in this way, it will become an adventure, not an ordeal.

Visualization frees the mind from its shackles.

Successful managers know why their employees resist change, and help them to prepare inwardly long before it happens. A vision should not just exist in the mind of one person: as many people as possible should be able to contribute to it so that it can be shared by everyone in the organization.

Exercise 19: Preparing for change:

List five situations in which you could have prepared yourself and other people for change.

a

b.

c.

d.

e.

Think of an important project in which you'll have to prepare yourself and your team members for change. List five ways in which you might do this so that they actually look forward to it.

Project:

a

b.

c.

d.

e.

7.4 Summary of chapter 7

Only those who are themselves motivated have the strength and charisma to motivate others. The skills we've explored in this module will help you to develop your potential and make use of the creative tensions within you. But remember that pressurizing other people in an attempt to motivate them will not work, and that includes trying to get people to do things they're quite simply incapable of. This applies as much to you as it does to other people.

8 - Self-appreciation – moving to the next level.

In this chapter, you'll learn how to use auto-suggestion to increase your self-esteem. You'll also gain an understanding of how you engage in a constant dialog with yourself, and learn to exert a positive influence on this dialog.

8.1 Developing high self-esteem

When your unconscious receives a message, it accepts it as the literal truth. The way in which you engage in dialog with yourself therefore creates a particular picture of reality in your unconscious.

If you tell yourself often enough "I'm stupid", you'll eventually start to act stupid. This is known as auto-suggestion.

Remember the following formula:

P x V = RU

Picture x Vividness = Reality in the Unconscious.

If you picture a situation so vividly that you can actually experience the same feeling that you would in reality, then it will become a reality in your unconscious.

For example, a lot of children feel ill at the very mention of spinach, not because they've ever tried it themselves but because others have told them it's revolting. They imagine and internalize this "truth", and decide they can't stomach it.

Auto-suggestion of this kind can either reduce or increase your self-esteem.

Increased self-esteem isn't something you can be taught, or which you suddenly decide to have. You can't just go to bed one night saying "When I wake up tomorrow, I'm going to have greater self-esteem." It's something you have to work on, and which requires a deliberate effort. Auto-suggestion is a constant process, controlled from inside by the self.

Start by developing a defense mechanism against other people's destructive statements. If you pay too much attention to these they can set up a process of negative auto-suggestion, and it takes a high degree of self-esteem simply to reject them out of hand.

But each time you politely reject negative comments made against yourself and other people, you'll feel that much more positive about yourself.

So how do you point out others' mistakes without injuring their self-esteem?

People with low self-esteem are fragile. If you're managing people like this, you're responsible for them just as you are for your own children.

It's important to be clear and unambiguous in drawing attention to any shortcomings. Say something like: "You're a first-class member of the team. I'll tell you when you're doing a good job, but I'll also tell you when you're not — that's what I'm here for."

And there are lots of ways of getting the point across without belittling people. You could say, "You're not performing to your usual high standards. I know you're capable of much better than this." Or "I'd rather you didn't do that. It's not the kind of thing I see you doing." The possibilities are endless.

A man cannot strengthen his weaknesses by weakening his strengths. He cannot build character by taking the initiative away from others. In the long term, he cannot help others by doing for them what they can and should be doing for themselves.

Abraham Lincoln

Exercise 20: Auto-suggestion/ Self talk:

Imagine someone denigrates you in the same way as you sometimes denigrate yourself. Would you want to be friends with them? Can you think of any examples where you have put yourself down?

Exercise 21: Auto-suggestion:

List five areas in which you could make more positive use of auto-suggestion.

a

b.

c.

d.

e.

8.2 High self-esteem and high performance

When members of your team do something good, give them constructive feedback immediately. As a visionary, it's your job to show reinforcing behavior.

And when they get things wrong, tell them in a way that won't injure their pride. This isn't just a matter of being kind to people: it's also about preserving their self-respect in order to maximize their performance. Don't take away their dignity, because dignity is something that everyone is entitled to. And use auto-suggestion not only to increase your self-esteem, but also to learn more effective ways of talking to other people.

Remember that people with low self-esteem feel threatened by those with high self-esteem. They react by finding fault, being pernickety, and constantly emphasizing that they're in charge.

Look around at the people in your own organization. Do you have people with low self-esteem playing management roles and setting objectives? If so, maybe it's time for change.

Don't let business problems turn into personal conflicts. And remember that if you feel good about yourself, you can make other people feel good about themselves.

8.3 Summary of chapter 8

Auto-suggestion is a very effective way of achieving high self-esteem and high performance both from yourself and those around you. Think positively about yourself, tell yourself that you're good, and start using auto-suggestion to move your life in the direction you want it to go. And remember that both at work and in your personal life, sarcasm and denigration are no way to get the best out of other people. Look for ways of improving your self-esteem without putting other people down.

9 - Visions of success

In this chapter, you'll build on what you've learned already to develop clear visions that will provide a driving force on the road to success.

The essence of management lies in having a vision. You must clearly formulate this vision at every available opportunity. If you're singing your own praises, you mustn't whisper!

Father Theodore Hesburgh,
Former president of Notre Dame University

9.1 Visions

A vision is the embodiment of your highest values, aspirations and goals. It inspires you to achieve your full potential, and provides a way of overcoming your fears and looking to the future, not the past or the present.

The reasonable person adapts himself to the world; the unreasonable person insists on trying to adapt the world to him. So all progress depends on unreasonable people.

George Bernard Shaw

9.2 The difference between goals and visions

Goals are often set on the basis of known limits; in other words, on what people are already able to do or which can be precisely estimated. This stifles creativity.

Visions are much better at motivating people, because they are not constrained by specific limits.

The managers of two competing hotels wanted to increase the number of repeat bookings, which stood at 5%. One group of managers was asked to set a target which they thought was realistic. They agreed that 7% was realistic, and they achieved it.

The managers of the other hotel were asked to set the ideal percentage as their target. They decided that 55% would be ideal, and achieved 42 percent!

During the process of developing a vision, people can come to understand what they really want, regardless of whether it seems possible or not at the time.

A vision involves envisaging an ideal reality and then building a bridge from the current situation to the desired one.

Of course there will be problems to solve along the way, but because there are no limits the process is more creative and rewarding.

Exercise 22: Your personal vision

Think about an area of your life that needs change. Develop a vision of the end result that you want to achieve, based not on what you think is feasible but on what you really want. Express this vision in the form of a single, powerful paragraph, using the present tense and the first person singular.

My vision:

9.3 How to make your vision a reality.

This section describes how to turn your vision into reality, step by step. It's very important to follow each of this these steps carefully. This is not just an academic exercise, but a process you should put your body and soul into.

9.3.1. Laying the foundations

1. Create a picture of what you really want to achieve.

Think about your own organization. What works well, and what could work better? Based on the answers to these questions, what do you see as being the ideal future for the organization?

2. Be creative.

Look at every possible solution, no matter how silly it may seem. Let your imagination fly off at all sorts of tangents, and take a holistic view rather than getting too focused on detail. Write your ideas down.

3. Get help from other people.

And that means everyone! Talk to your bosses, colleagues, clients, suppliers, your spouse or partner, the milkman. Ask them what they think is the best approach. Is it the same as yours, or completely different?

4. Get your thoughts in order.

Produce a written summary of your own and others' ideas, and then test them out on colleagues or a mentor.

9.3.2 Formulating your own vision

1. Express your vision in personal terms

Use the first person singular. You can't develop a vision for someone else, because it wouldn't be effective for them. For example, you can't say "I want my husband/wife/partner to be more patient and spend more time with the family," because that won't change them in the slightest.

However, if you say something like "I'm becoming more caring and loving towards other people, and this is bringing my family closer together," this will probably rub off on your partner as well.

2. Make it positive

Concentrate not on the behavior you're trying to avoid, but on what you want to achieve. Don't say: "I'm going to give up smoking and drinking and stop being such a couch potato." Say: "I'm healthy and I get plenty of exercise."

3. Use the present tense

A vision is essentially a picture of the way you want to be, and what you want your unconscious to see as a reality. Your unconscious will only respond to statements in the present tense and, as we've already seen, it doesn't distinguish between fact and fiction. If you make a personal, positive statement in the first person singular and the present tense, your unconscious will accept it at face value.

So, for example, if you say, "I'm a successful marathon runner", your unconscious will accept this as a fact. This creates a cognitive dissonance, in other words a tension between the statement that you're a successful marathon runner and the fact that you're not. This tension should give you the drive to become one.

However, if you were to say: "I'm going to run the New York City Marathon in two years' time", this would be a goal, not a vision. There would be no tension between the image of the current situation in your unconscious and your current external reality, and thus none of the drive and energy required to make the goal a reality.

Current reality → **Tension** → **Vision**

4. Make it clear what you've already achieved

Say: "I'm a highly creative electrical engineer," not: "I have the potential to be a highly creative electrical engineer."

If your unconscious accepts that you are one and feedback from the actual reality makes it clear that you're not, this will significantly increase your desire to achieve change. Saying "I have the potential to be" implies that you might become that way at some unspecified future date, and therefore creates little or no tension. You must make it appear to your unconscious that you've already achieved the end result.

5. Avoid making comparisons

Decide what is best for you, and you alone. You can't find this out by comparing yourself to other people; even their best may not be good enough for you. The only person you should be competing against is yourself, though there's nothing wrong with using others as an example by taking the best of their ideas and making these your own.

6. Don't use negative statements

Your vision shouldn't include any negative words, because your unconscious can't cope with them. They will also make you feel negative and drain your energy.

7. Use dynamic, emotional words

Words with connotations of action and emotion will help you to realize your vision. The stronger the emotions, the more creative tension they will generate.

8. Be specific

Make sure your vision gives you a clear picture in your mind. For example, if you want to be richer, you might imagine yourself as a millionaire. But if you have difficulty picturing what being a millionaire is like, you could visualize something more tangible, such as trebling your income.

9. Be realistic

Don't strive for perfection. Words like "always" and "never" create unrealistic expectations.

10. Be consistent

If you have more than one vision, make sure they're not contradictory. A vision must serve a core goal that is rooted in your central motivation for living.

Exercise 23: Formulating visions:

List three areas of your personal life in which you'd like to achieve growth.

a _____

_____

_____

b. _____

_____

_____

c. _____

_____

_____

Using the ten guidelines above, write down a strong, clear vision story for each of these areas. (At least one paragraph)!

a _____

_____

_____

_____

b. _____

_____

_____

_____

c. _____

_____

_____

Rewrite the vision that you wrote down in exercise 22 to take the ten guidelines into account.

Remember : Always relate your vision in the form of a powerful story, the take is much stronger.

9.4 Summary of chapter 9

If you've worked your way through all the previous chapters and done the exercises, you should have the skills required to develop your own vision. Doing so may be a long and very difficult task, but don't worry; Rome wasn't built in a day. No matter how much you practice, it will always require a huge amount of effort and concentration.

I suggest putting your visions to one side and forgetting them for a day or two. Then read through this chapter again, select your most important vision and rewrite it, ignoring the one you produced the first time around. If there are big differences between the two, it may be that there are still some skills you need to develop, in which case you should re-read the appropriate chapter of the book.

10 - Personal and organizational visions

In this last and very important chapter you'll learn how to involve other people in your vision, and how to mobilize sufficient energy in them to help you realize it together.

10.1 Personal and organizational visions

A realistic vision is one that is both challenging and feasible. It must leave a certain amount of scope for imagination, and must be difficult, but not impossible to achieve. It will probably contain some abstract principles such as quality, performance and service which will inspire people to perform well, but at the same time it must be firmly grounded in reality, because otherwise there is no real point in trying to achieve it.

Both individual and corporate visions involve a gap between the reality and the objective that creates tension, drive and energy.

Tension, which is an important component of the creative process, is normally released in one of the following two ways:

1. Sufficient energy is generated to change the current reality into the new and desired reality described in the vision

2. The vision is changed so that it matches the current reality.

In an organization, people will often respond emotionally to the expression of a vision. It makes them feel insecure and inferior, and they will try to overcome this feeling as quickly as possible, which means they become more focused on the current reality than the vision.

The result is that the organization ends up with a compromise between the two.

A visionary organization refuses to let go of its vision of the future. This determines everything it does, and its visible commitment gives it a clear sense of direction.

Take the Apollo project, for example. In 1969, the Apollo team was planning a landing on the moon in the face of seemingly insuperable obstacles. Because most of the people involved in the project were committed to its vision of putting a man on the moon in that year, they were able to overcome their problems and achieve the vision. Without this commitment, they would not have been able to achieve such enormous creativity and groundbreaking technological progress.

All visions and communication are useless if they do not lead to action.

Donella and Dennis Meadows

Exercise 24: Turning work visions into reality:

1. Write down two visions that exist in your workplace.

a _____
_____
_____
_____

b. _____
_____
_____
_____

2. Decide whether these visions have been realized or are still in progress.

a _____
_____
_____
_____

b. _____
_____
_____
_____

3. Write down the five main reasons why they are, or are not, being achieved.

Reasons why vision is being achieved

a

b.

c.

d.

e.

Reasons why vision is not being achieved

a

b.

c.

d.

e.

10.2 Alignment and agreement

As we've already seen in earlier chapters, every individual has a strong sense of the central motivating purpose of their life.

Many philosophers have asserted that personal drive, energy and fulfillment are achieved by acting in harmony with one's central motivation. If you have a strong enough sense of this, you can use it to develop the skills you need to achieve your purpose in life.

Conversely, if you've identified this purpose and live in accordance with it, you've achieved alignment with yourself.

A visionary manager has a clear idea of the organization's purpose, and a clear vision which brings everyone involved into alignment with it.

We define "alignment" as a situation where every member of the team is able to freely harness their own energy in the service of the greater w

It occurs when the team members see the organization's purpose as an extension of their own. They identify with it, and are willing to take responsibility for its success. Mutual support is essential, based on the realization that everyone is a part of a larger whole.

10.3 The difference between alignment and agreement

Alignment relates more to people's mental attitudes to the organization's purpose and visions, whereas agreement is about the mechanisms of setting objectives.

If a group of people agree about something, all they're saying is "we share the same good ideas."

If a group of people are aligned with one another, they are more likely to keep to any agreements they make, because everyone feels wholly committed to a shared purpose.

10.4. How a successful leader creates alignment

1. By co-creating effective visions!

Effective visions inspire people and demand that they give of their best. Everyone has a clear idea of the organization's purpose, and the vision represents a clear challenge and reflects a healthy understanding of people. A vision should be a safe anchor in stormy seas. As many people as possible should contribute to the creation of the vision story since an organization with a co-created vision does not have to exert control over its employees; because they are able to act on their own responsibility. It prepares people for the future, without forgetting the past.

Exercise 25: Formulating organizational visions

Formulate the Vision concept

Read through the visions you noted down in earlier exercises, and based on these write down what you've learned about alignment and effective visions. Now create a powerful storyline for an effective organizational vision. Tell this vision story to somebody else, and explain why you've chosen this particular form of words.

Ask them for feedback both on the nature of the vision itself and the way in which you express it. What are their thoughts, and, perhaps more importantly, their feelings.

2. By testing out the visions.

Before you share your vision stories with others, test out every aspect of them with all the people involved. Decide who you want to share them with, and why. Don't allow them to become just empty words by not living them out in your own life.

3. By talking about them.

Use every opportunity to talk about your visions. Identify everyday activities by team members that support them, and tell them why.

4. By being emotionally committed to them.

A manager's visions or plans are compellingly attractive to other people. Intensity and commitment are a magnetic combination. People with strong personalities do not have to force others to take notice: they concentrate so much on what they are doing that they become immersed in it, like a child building a castle in a sandpit that draws others beneath its spell.

Warren Bennis

5. Through leading by example.

Set a good example by putting aside time each day to realize your vision. People will find it easier to support if they can see that you're devoting a great deal of time to it.

Exercise 26: Leading by example:

List five possible situations where you could be an example to others.

a

b.

c.

d.

e.

Exercise 27: Putting visions into action:

Look back at the vision you wrote down in exercise 25, and think of at least seven different ways in which you can be seen to be spending time on realizing it.

a

b.

c.

d.

e.

e.

e.

Discuss your answers to exercises 26 and 27 with someone else. Do they find your ideas inspiring.

6. By using symbols.

Tell stories and use metaphors and analogies to focus people on your vision. Everyone loves a good story.

Exercise 28: Using symbols

Meetings and other forms of interaction with people are full of symbols. These tell you a lot about the people involved, e.g. where the meeting is held, the food served, etc.

Think about the symbolic value of some of the everyday things you do. Do people leave their doors open? Does everyone wear a tie? Who parks their car where? When two people meet, who says hello first? Are team members asked to do things, or told to? Do they enjoy themselves?

How can you use symbols in the service of your vision?

7. They keep working on their visions.

Use guidelines 1-7 above to work on developing a corporate culture that embodies your vision. Bear this in mind while you do the next exercise.

Exercise 29: Vision as story:

Think of a new way to turn your vision into a story, and tell it to someone you haven't told about your vision yet.

Obtain feedback about their thoughts and feelings!

If something has not been talked about, it has not happened.
Only words give things reality

Oscar Wilde

10.5 Visions and intuition : A living vision

Once managers and team members are aware of the organization's purpose and have formulated a vision, and once suitably skilled people are working in harmony together, they will develop a greater ability to take decisions intuitively.

Experience has shown that the most successful managers are those who think holistically and intuitively, and who rely on hunches to solve problems that are too complex for rational analysis.

The most convincing visions arise when people understand the purpose of the organization and have a clear idea of the future. Intuition gives a greater sense of purpose and raises the art of prediction to an altogether higher level. A vision that is emotionally convincing can never be created using rational intellect.

The more intuitive an organization is, the easier it becomes to bring employees' intuitions into line with management's vision.

Because individuals have an intuitive understanding of others, it becomes much easier for them to work together.

The American basketball star Bill Russell describes his experience of harmony and intuition as follows. "Again and again, the atmosphere at a Celtics game would warm up so that it was no longer a physical or even a mental game — it was pure magic. The feeling is not easy to describe, and I certainly never talked about it during the game. When something like that happened, I could feel my game being raised to a whole new level. It didn't happen often, and it lasted for varying periods of time from five minutes to an entire half or longer. Sometimes it wouldn't happen for three or four plays. This feeling gripped not just me and the other Celtics players, but the opposing team and even the umpires.

"At this very special level, strange things can happen. Every stage of the game was incredibly competitive, and yet I never felt like a competitor — which speaks for itself. I drove myself to the limits and my lungs to bursting, but I never felt pain. The game was so fast that every ball and every pass came as a surprise, and yet nothing could surprise me. It was almost as though we were playing in a time warp. At times like these I could almost feel how the next play would develop and where the next throw would come from.

"Even before the other team put the ball into play I could feed it coming so strongly that I wanted to shout to my teammates "Here it comes!" — but of course I knew that if I did actually shout out, it would all happen differently. My suspicions were always right, and I always had the feeling that I knew not only all the Celtics players inside and out, but also all the opposing players — and they all knew me. There were many moments in my career when I felt emotional or ecstatically happy, but at moments like these a shiver would run down my spine.

Sometimes this feeling went on until the end of the game, and when this happened I simply didn't care who had won. I can honestly say these were the only times it didn't matter to me. I'm not saying I was just being a good loser and saying 'I gave my best, and that's what counts.' On the five or six occasions that the match ended on this special level, in the truest sense of the word I didn't care who had won. Even when we lost, I always felt as free as a bird."

Exercise 30: Establishing contact and alignment

Sit opposite someone you trust. Close your eyes and spend three minutes or so trying to feel your way into their mind and establish intuitive contact with them. Then open your eyes and tell them how you felt and what you thought.

Ask for feedback about what you've said.

10.6 Conclusion

Congratulations! By now, you should understand yourself a bit better!

If you keep working your vision stories you will become part of the 80% of all the people who have seriously embraced this process and have experienced positive life-changing events as a result!

And don't forget, keep your visions up to date if you want to achieve lasting success.

About the Author

Albert Zandvoort BA, MA,MSc, DLit et Phil, PhD

Dr. Albert Zandvoort is the Academic Director of the Witten School of Management at the University of Witten Herdecke in Germany, the former director of the Ashridge Leadership Centre and an Associate Member of the Ashridge Business School (UK) faculty. He is also a visiting professor at Oxford and HEC in Paris.

His interests range from leadership to performance management, large systems change, lifelong learning, personal skills development, scenario building and team building. Albert also has a keen interest in executive coaching and is working with a number of senior executives on their organizational and leadership issues.

Before joining academia, Albert held executive positions at Lufthansa, T-Mobile in Germany and Transnet in South Africa. He has consulted for major organizations in Europe, the USA and also to the Russian Academy of Sciences. Some current clients are Saint Gobain in France, Phillips in the Netherlands, Bayer, Axel Springer Publishers and Merck in Germany.

Albert has written extensively on Leadership, HR and political consulting, training and development and psychotherapy.

Albert is also a psychotherapist in private practice in London and special advisor to the UK based Charity Drugfam.